FORAGER'S HARVEST RECIPES COOKBOOK

The Ultimate Guide to Cooking Edible Wild Greens, Berries, Fruits, Seeds and Nuts

By: Botanic Delights

Copyright © 2023 by Botanic Delights

All rights reserved.
No part of this publication may be reproduced, distributed, or transmitted in any form or by any means, including photocopying, recording, or other electronic or mechanical methods, without the prior written permission of the publisher, except in the case of brief quotations embodied in critical reviews and certain other noncommercial uses permitted by copyright law.

TABLE OF CONTENT

How to Use This Book................ 5
Introduction............................. 7
WILD GREENS....................... 8
    Wild Green Salad............................8
    Sauteed Wild Greens....................... 9
    Wild Green Pesto............................9
    Wild Green Smoothie..................... 10
    Wild Green Stir-Fry........................11
UNDERGROUND VEGETABLES.13
    Roasted Root Vegetables................ 13
    Mashed Root Vegetables..................13
    Vegetable Stew with Underground Vegetables....................... 14
    Root Vegetable Fries......................15
    Root Vegetable Hash..................... 16
    Root Vegetable Gratin.....................17
WILD FRUITS AND BERRIES.... 19
    Wild Berry Smoothie Bowl............. 19
    Wild Berry Jam............................. 20
    Wild Fruit Salad............................ 20
    Wild Berry Crumble........................21
    Wild Fruit Infused Water...............22

Wild Berry Pancakes....................... 23
Wild Fruit Salsa.............................. 24
WILD SEEDS AND GRAINS....... 25
Quinoa and Wild Seed Salad........... 25
Wild Seed Energy Balls................... 25
Wild Seed and Grain Bread............. 26
Wild Seed and Grain Granola......... 28
Wild Seed and Grain Salad..............29
WILD NUTS............................. 30
Wild Nut Butter...............................30
Wild Nut Trail Mix.......................... 31
Wild Nut-Crusted Fish or Chicken.. 31
Wild Nut and Green Salad.............. 32
Wild Nut-Crusted Goat Cheese....... 33
Wild Nut Energy Bars..................... 34
Conclusion............................... 36

How to Use This Book

Congratulations on acquiring this forager's harvest recipes cookbook! Here are some tips on how to make the most of this book and enhance your culinary journey with edible wild plants:

1. Read the Introduction: Start by reading the introduction, as it provides an overview of the book's content, introduces the concept of foraging, and highlights the nutritional benefits of edible wild plants.

2. Recipe Selection: Browse through the recipes within each section and choose the ones that pique your interest. The recipes range from appetizers and main courses to desserts and beverages, providing a diverse array of options to suit your taste preferences.

3. Ingredient Availability: Keep in mind that the availability of specific wild plants may vary depending on your geographical location and the season. Some ingredients may be more readily accessible in certain regions or during specific times of the year. Make note of alternative options suggested within the recipes if specific ingredients are not accessible to you.

4. Adaptation and Creativity: Feel free to adapt the recipes to suit your preferences and experiment with flavors. Foraged ingredients often offer unique tastes and textures, so don't be afraid to get creative and add your personal touch to the dishes.

5. Measurement Conversions: The book may include measurements in various systems (e.g., metric and imperial). Familiarize yourself with the conversions or use a conversion tool to ensure accurate measurements.

Introduction

The Forager's Harvest Recipes Cookbook is a culinary treasure, beckoning you to embrace a nourishing and sustainable lifestyle. Amidst a world of processed foods, it offers a gateway to reconnect with nature's bountiful offerings. This cookbook holds the key to transforming wild plants into delectable dishes that tantalize the taste buds and nourish the body.

Beyond flavor, it unveils a wealth of health benefits, with nutrient-rich ingredients bolstering your well-being. But it's more than just recipes—it rekindles our ancestral bond with nature, promoting responsible foraging and sustainable practices. With each dish, we foster a deeper appreciation for the environment, fostering harmony on our plates.

Join the ranks of modern-day foragers and eco-conscious individuals, embarking on a remarkable journey guided by this invaluable cookbook. Discover a tastier, healthier, and more sustainable way of living—one delectable recipe at a time.

WILD GREENS

Wild Green Salad

Ingredients: A mix of wild greens (dandelion, stinging nettle, purslane), cherry tomatoes, cucumber slices, radishes, feta cheese, toasted nuts (walnuts or hazelnuts), and a vinaigrette dressing.

Instructions:
- Wash the wild greens thoroughly and pat them dry.
- Tear or chop the greens into bite-sized pieces and place them in a large salad bowl.
- Add cherry tomatoes, cucumber slices, radishes, crumbled feta cheese, and toasted nuts to the bowl.
- In a separate container, prepare your favorite vinaigrette dressing.
- Toss the salad carefully to evenly distribute the dressing over all of the ingredients.
- Serve the wild green salad as a refreshing and nutritious side dish or main course.

Sauteed Wild Greens

Ingredients: Wild greens (such as lambsquarters, chicory, or mustard greens), olive oil, garlic, salt, and pepper.

Instructions:
- Wash the wild greens thoroughly and remove any tough stems or damaged leaves.
- Over medium heat, warm the olive oil in the pan.
- Add minced garlic to the pan and sauté until fragrant.
- Add the wild greens to the pan, season with salt and pepper, and toss them gently.
- Cook the greens for a few minutes until they wilt and become tender.
- Remove from heat and serve the sautéed wild greens as a flavorful and nutritious side dish.

Wild Green Pesto

Ingredients: Wild greens (such as nettle, sorrel, or basil leaves), pine nuts (or any nuts of your choice), garlic cloves, grated Parmesan cheese, olive oil, salt, and pepper.

Instructions:
- Blanch the wild greens in boiling water for a

minute, then drain and rinse them with cold water.
- In a food processor, combine the blanched wild greens, pine nuts, garlic cloves, grated Parmesan cheese, salt, and pepper.
- Blend the ingredients while gradually adding olive oil until you achieve a smooth and creamy consistency.
- If necessary, taste and adjust the seasoning.
- Use the wild green pesto as a spread on sandwiches, toss it with pasta, or enjoy it as a dip or sauce for various dishes.

Wild Green Smoothie

Ingredients: Wild greens (such as spinach, lambsquarters, or dandelion greens), ripe bananas, frozen berries (blueberries, strawberries), almond milk (or any milk of your choice), honey or maple syrup (optional).

Instructions:
- Wash the wild greens thoroughly and remove any tough stems or damaged leaves.
- Place the wild greens, ripe bananas, frozen berries, almond milk, and sweetener (if desired) into a blender.
- Until the mixture is smooth and creamy, blend the ingredients quickly.

- Taste and adjust the sweetness or consistency by adding more sweetener or almond milk as needed.
- Pour the wild green smoothie into glasses and serve it chilled as a refreshing and nutrient-packed beverage.

Wild Green Stir-Fry

Ingredients: Wild greens (such as amaranth leaves, watercress, or beet greens), mixed vegetables (bell peppers, mushrooms, carrots), tofu or your choice of protein, soy sauce, sesame oil, garlic, ginger, chili flakes (optional), and cooked rice or noodles.

Instructions:
- Wash the wild greens thoroughly and chop them into manageable pieces.
- Cut the mixed vegetables, such as bell peppers, mushrooms, and carrots, into thin slices or bite-sized pieces.
- Drain and cube any tofu you plan to use.
- In a sizable skillet or wok, warm the sesame oil over medium-high heat.
- Add minced garlic, grated ginger, and chili flakes (if desired) to the skillet and sauté for a minute until fragrant.

- Add the mixed vegetables and tofu to the skillet and stir-fry for a few minutes until they begin to soften.
- Add the wild greens to the skillet and continue stir-frying for another few minutes until the greens wilt and become tender.
- Pour in a splash of soy sauce and toss everything together to coat evenly.
- Adjust the seasoning to taste and remove from heat.
- Serve the wild green stir-fry over cooked rice or noodles for a satisfying and flavorful meal. These recipes provide a range of delicious ways to incorporate wild greens into your culinary repertoire. Feel free to adjust the ingredients and seasonings according to your preferences and enjoy the unique flavors and nutritional benefits of wild greens in your meals!

UNDERGROUND VEGETABLES

Roasted Root Vegetables

Ingredients: Underground vegetables such as carrots, parsnips, sweet potatoes, beets, and onions, olive oil, salt, and pepper.

Instructions:
- Preheat the oven to 425°F (220°C).
- Peel and chop the underground vegetables into bite-sized pieces.
- Toss the vegetables with olive oil, salt, and pepper in a mixing bowl until well coated.
- On a baking sheet, arrange the vegetables in a single layer.
- Roast in the preheated oven for about 30-40 minutes, or until they are golden brown and tender.
- Serve the roasted root vegetables as a delicious and nutritious side dish.

Mashed Root Vegetables

Ingredients: Underground vegetables such as potatoes, rutabagas, turnips, or celeriac, butter, milk (or cream), salt, and pepper.

Instructions:
- Peel and cut the underground vegetables into chunks.
- Put them in a big pot, then fill it with water.
- Bring the water to a boil and cook the vegetables until they are tender when pierced with a fork.
- Drain the cooked vegetables and return them to the pot.
- Add the appropriate amounts of butter, milk (or cream), salt, and pepper.
- Mash the vegetables with a potato masher or blend them with a hand mixer until smooth and creamy.
- Adjust the seasoning if needed and serve the mashed root vegetables as a comforting and flavorful side dish.

Vegetable Stew with Underground Vegetables

Ingredients: Underground vegetables such as potatoes, carrots, parsnips, celery root, onions, garlic, vegetable broth, herbs (such as thyme and rosemary), salt, and pepper.

Instructions:
- Peel and chop the underground vegetables into bite-sized pieces.
- Over medium heat, warm the olive oil in a big pot or Dutch oven.
- Add chopped onions and minced garlic to the pot and sauté until they are softened and fragrant.
- Add the chopped underground vegetables to the pot and stir to coat them with the onions and garlic.
- Pour in vegetable broth to cover the vegetables and bring it to a boil.
- When the vegetables are ready, lower the heat, cover the pan, and simmer for 20 to 30 minutes.
- Season the stew with herbs, salt, and pepper to taste.
- Serve the vegetable stew hot, garnished with fresh herbs if desired.

Root Vegetable Fries

Ingredients: Underground vegetables such as carrots, sweet potatoes, parsnips, or beets, olive oil, salt, and spices (such as paprika, cumin, or garlic powder).

Instructions:

- A baking sheet should be lined with parchment paper and the oven should be preheated to 425°F (220°C).
- Peel the underground vegetables and cut them into thin, fry-like strips.
- Place the vegetable strips in a mixing bowl and drizzle with olive oil.
- Sprinkle with salt, spices, and any other desired seasonings, then toss to coat evenly.
- Arrange the vegetable strips in a single layer on the prepared baking sheet.
- Bake the fries for 20 to 25 minutes, tossing them halfway through, or until they are crispy and golden brown.
- Serve the root vegetable fries as a healthier alternative to traditional fries, with your favorite dipping sauces or as a side dish to complement a main meal.

Root Vegetable Hash

Ingredients: Underground vegetables such as potatoes, sweet potatoes, turnips, or beets, onions, bell peppers, garlic, olive oil, salt, pepper, and optional herbs (such as thyme or rosemary).

Instructions:

- Peel and chop the underground vegetables into small, even-sized cubes.
- Slice the garlic, and dice the bell peppers and onions.
- In a skillet over medium heat, warm the olive oil.
Add the onions and bell peppers to the skillet and sauté until they are softened.
- Add the chopped underground vegetables and minced garlic to the skillet, season with salt, pepper, and optional herbs, and stir to combine.
- Cook the hash mixture for about 15-20 minutes, stirring occasionally, until the vegetables are tender and lightly browned.
- Adjust the seasoning if needed, and serve the root vegetable hash as a delicious and hearty breakfast or brunch option.

Root Vegetable Gratin

Ingredients: Underground vegetables such as potatoes, turnips, or sweet potatoes, heavy cream, grated cheese (such as Gruyère or cheddar), garlic, thyme, salt, and pepper.

Instructions:
- Peel the underground vegetables and slice them into thin rounds.

- Preheat the oven to 375°F (190°C) and grease a baking dish.
- Layer the vegetable slices in the baking dish, alternating different types if desired.
- In a small saucepan, heat the heavy cream, minced garlic, thyme, salt, and pepper until it simmers.
- Pour the cream mixture over the layered vegetables, ensuring they are well-coated.
- Over the gratin, top with the grated cheese.
- Bake the dish for 30 minutes with the foil covering. Then remove the foil and bake for an additional 20-25 minutes until the top is golden and the vegetables are tender.
- Allow the gratin to cool slightly before serving, as it will be piping hot.
- Serve the root vegetable gratin as a comforting and indulgent side dish for special occasions or as a hearty vegetarian main course.

WILD FRUITS AND BERRIES

Wild Berry Smoothie Bowl

Ingredients: Mixed wild berries (such as blackberries, raspberries, and blueberries), ripe bananas, Greek yogurt, honey or maple syrup (optional), granola, and assorted toppings (such as sliced almonds, chia seeds, or shredded coconut).

Instructions:
- In a blender, combine the wild berries, ripe bananas, Greek yogurt, and sweetener (if desired).
- Blend until smooth and creamy.
- Pour the smoothie into a bowl.
- Top with granola and assorted toppings of your choice.
- Enjoy the vibrant and nutritious wild berry smoothie bowl for breakfast or a refreshing snack.

Wild Berry Jam

Ingredients: Mixed wild berries (such as strawberries, blackberries, or huckleberries), sugar, lemon juice.

Instructions:
- Wash the wild berries and remove any stems or leaves.
- The berries, sugar, and lemon juice should all be combined in a sizable saucepan.
- Stirring occasionally, cook the mixture over medium heat until it boils.
- Reduce the heat to low and simmer for about 20-30 minutes, or until the berries break down and the mixture thickens.
- Remove from heat and let the jam cool.
- Transfer the jam into sterilized jars and seal tightly.
- Store in the refrigerator and enjoy the homemade wild berry jam on toast, pancakes, or as a topping for desserts.

Wild Fruit Salad

Ingredients: Assorted wild fruits (such as elderberries, serviceberries, or wild plums), fresh mint leaves, lime juice, honey or agave syrup (optional).

Instructions:
- Wash and prepare the wild fruits, removing any stems or seeds.
- The fruits should be put in a big bowl.
- In a separate small bowl, whisk together lime juice and honey or agave syrup (if desired) to make the dressing.
- Drizzle the dressing over the fruits and gently toss to coat.
- Tear fresh mint leaves and sprinkle them over the salad for added freshness.
- Prior to serving, give the flavors time to blend.
- Serve the refreshing wild fruit salad as a light and healthy dessert or snack.

Wild Berry Crumble

Ingredients: Mixed wild berries (such as blackberries, raspberries, or wild strawberries), flour, oats, brown sugar, butter, cinnamon, and optional vanilla ice cream or whipped cream for serving.

Instructions:
- Preheat the oven to 375°F (190°C).
- In a bowl, combine the wild berries with a sprinkle of flour and toss gently to coat.
- Place the berries in an ovenproof dish.

- Combine the flour, oats, brown sugar, and cinnamon in another basin.
- Use a pastry cutter or your fingertips to incorporate the chilled butter until the mixture resembles coarse crumbs.
- The crumble mixture should be uniformly distributed over the berries in the baking dish.
- Bake in the preheated oven for about 30-35 minutes, or until the top is golden brown and the berries are bubbling.
- Take it out of the oven, then allow it to cool somewhat.
- Serve the warm wild berry crumble with a scoop of vanilla ice cream or a dollop of whipped cream.

Wild Fruit Infused Water

Ingredients: Assorted wild fruits (such as berries, sliced citrus fruits, or sliced apples), fresh mint leaves, filtered water.

Instructions:
- Wash and prepare the wild fruits, removing any stems or seeds.
- Place the fruits and fresh mint leaves in a pitcher.
- Fill the pitcher with filtered water.
- Stir gently to release the flavors of the fruits and mint.

- Refrigerate the infused water for at least 2-4 hours, or overnight, to allow the flavors to infuse.
- Serve the refreshing wild fruit-infused water chilled, garnished with additional fresh mint leaves if desired.

Wild Berry Pancakes

Ingredients: Mixed wild berries (such as blueberries, blackberries, or cranberries), pancake mix, milk (or plant-based milk), eggs (or egg substitute), butter or oil for cooking, maple syrup for serving.

Instructions:
- Wash and prepare the wild berries, removing any stems or leaves.
- In a mixing bowl, prepare the pancake batter according to the instructions on the pancake mix, using milk and eggs.
- Gently fold in the wild berries into the pancake batter.
- Heat a non-stick skillet or griddle over medium heat and melt a small amount of butter or oil.
- Pour a ladleful of the pancake batter onto the skillet, spreading it slightly with the back of the ladle.

- Cook until bubbles form on the surface of the pancake, then flip and cook the other side until golden brown.
- Repeat the process with the remaining batter. Serve the delicious wild berry pancakes stacked high, drizzled with maple syrup.

Wild Fruit Salsa

Ingredients: Assorted wild fruits (such as strawberries, blueberries, or kiwi), red onion, jalapeño (optional), fresh lime juice, cilantro leaves, salt, and pepper.

Instructions:
- Wash and prepare the wild fruits, removing any stems or seeds.
- Dice them into small pieces.
- Finely chop the red onion and jalapeño (if using), removing the seeds for milder heat.
- In a bowl, combine the diced wild fruits, red onion, jalapeño, fresh lime juice, and chopped cilantro leaves.
- To taste, add salt and pepper to the food.
- Mix thoroughly and give the flavors time to mingle.
- Serve the vibrant and flavorful wild fruit salsa with tortilla chips, as a topping for grilled meats, or as a refreshing side dish.

WILD SEEDS AND GRAINS

Quinoa and Wild Seed Salad

Ingredients: Quinoa, mixed wild seeds (such as chia seeds, flaxseeds, or hemp seeds), mixed vegetables (such as diced bell peppers, cucumber, and cherry tomatoes), fresh herbs (such as parsley), olive oil, salt, pepper and lemon juice.

Instructions:
- Prepare the quinoa per the directions on the package, then let it cool.
- In a bowl, combine the cooked quinoa, mixed wild seeds, diced vegetables, and chopped herbs.
- Drizzle with lemon juice and olive oil, and season with salt and pepper.
- Toss everything together until well combined.
- Serve the quinoa and wild seed salad as a nutritious and flavorful side dish or light lunch.

Wild Seed Energy Balls

Ingredients: Mixed wild seeds (such as pumpkin seeds, sunflower seeds, and sesame seeds), dried fruits (such as dates or raisins), nut butter (such as almond or peanut butter), honey or maple syrup, shredded coconut (optional).

Instructions:
- In a food processor, combine the mixed wild seeds, dried fruits, nut butter, and sweetener.
- Pulse the mixture until a sticky dough is formed.
- Using your hands, form tiny balls out of the dough.
- You may roll the energy balls in shredded coconut for added texture and flavor.
- Place the energy balls on a baking sheet or plate and refrigerate for at least 30 minutes to firm up.
- Enjoy the homemade wild seed energy balls as a healthy and convenient snack on the go.

Wild Seed and Grain Bread

Ingredients: Mixed wild seeds (such as flaxseeds, poppy seeds, or sesame seeds), mixed grains (such as rolled oats, millet, or quinoa flakes), whole wheat flour, yeast, warm water, honey or maple syrup, salt, and olive oil.

Instructions:
- In a large mixing bowl, combine the mixed

wild seeds, mixed grains, whole wheat flour, and salt.
- Dissolve the yeast and sweetener in warm water and let it sit for a few minutes until frothy.
- Combine the dry ingredients with the yeast mixture and olive oil.
- Stir until a dough forms, then knead the dough on a lightly floured surface for about 5-10 minutes until smooth and elastic.
- Put the dough in a greased basin, cover it with a damp cloth, and let it rise in a warm location for about one to two hours, or until it has doubled in size.
- The dough should be pounded down and formed into a loaf.
- Place the loaf in a greased bread pan and let it rise for another 30-45 minutes until it rises above the rim of the pan.
- Preheat the oven to 375°F (190°C) and bake the bread for about 30-35 minutes until golden brown and sounds hollow when tapped on the bottom.
- Let the bread cool completely before cutting.
- Serve the delicious and nutritious wild seed and grain bread as a hearty accompaniment to soups, sandwiches, or enjoy it toasted with your favorite spreads.

Wild Seed and Grain Granola

Ingredients: Mixed wild seeds (such as pumpkin seeds, sunflower seeds, and chia seeds), mixed grains (such as rolled oats, quinoa flakes, or amaranth), nuts (such as almonds or walnuts), dried fruits (such as cranberries or apricots), honey or maple syrup, coconut oil, vanilla extract, cinnamon, and salt.

Instructions:
- Set a baking sheet on the oven's 325°F (160°C) setting and preheat the oven.
- In a large mixing bowl, combine the mixed wild seeds, mixed grains, nuts, and dried fruits.
- In a small saucepan, heat the honey or maple syrup, coconut oil, vanilla extract, cinnamon, and salt until melted and well combined.
- Pour the honey or maple syrup mixture over the dry ingredients and stir until everything is evenly coated.
- Spread the granola mixture in an even layer on the prepared baking sheet.
- Bake for about 25-30 minutes, stirring halfway through, until golden brown and fragrant.
- Remove from the oven and let the granola cool completely.
- Once cooled, break the granola into clusters.

- Store in an airtight container and enjoy the wild seed and grain granola as a nutritious breakfast cereal or as a topping for yogurt, smoothie bowls, or desserts.

Wild Seed and Grain Salad

Ingredients: Mixed wild seeds (such as hemp seeds, sesame seeds, or flaxseeds), mixed grains (such as bulgur wheat, quinoa, or barley), mixed vegetables (such as diced cucumbers, cherry tomatoes, and bell peppers), fresh herbs (such as parsley or mint), lemon juice, olive oil, salt, and pepper.

Instructions:
- Cook the mixed grains according to package instructions and let them cool.
- In a bowl, combine the cooked mixed grains, mixed wild seeds, diced vegetables, and chopped herbs.
- Drizzle with lemon juice and olive oil, and season with salt and pepper.
- Toss everything together until well combined.
- Let the flavors meld together for a few minutes before serving.
- Serve the wild seed and grain salad as a wholesome and satisfying side dish or light lunch option.

WILD NUTS

Wild Nut Butter

Ingredients: Assorted wild nuts (such as walnuts, pecans, or hazelnuts), salt (optional).

Instructions:
- Preheat the oven to 350°F (175°C) and spread the wild nuts on a baking sheet.
- Toast the nuts in the oven for about 10-15 minutes until they are fragrant and lightly browned.
- Remove the nuts from the oven and let them cool slightly.
- Place the toasted nuts in a food processor or high-speed blender.
- Process the nuts until they become creamy and smooth, scraping down the sides as needed.
- You may add a pinch of salt to enhance the flavor of the nut butter.
- Transfer the wild nut butter to a jar and store it in the refrigerator.
- Use the wild nut butter as a spread on toast, in smoothies, or as a versatile ingredient in both sweet and savory recipes.

Wild Nut Trail Mix

Ingredients: Assorted wild nuts (such as almonds, cashews, or Brazil nuts), dried fruits (such as cranberries, raisins, or cherries), seeds (such as pumpkin seeds or sunflower seeds), and optional additions like dark chocolate chips or coconut flakes.

Instructions:
- Roughly chop the wild nuts and combine them in a bowl with the dried fruits and seeds.
- Add any optional ingredients you desire, such as dark chocolate chips or coconut flakes.
- Toss everything together until well mixed.
- Transfer the wild nut trail mix to an airtight container or individual snack-sized bags.
- Enjoy the trail mix as a convenient and nutritious snack on the go or as a topping for yogurt, salads, or desserts.

Wild Nut-Crusted Fish or Chicken

Ingredients: Assorted wild nuts (such as pistachios, macadamia nuts, or almonds), fish fillets or chicken breasts, flour, eggs, olive oil, salt, and pepper.

Instructions:
- Set an empty baking sheet in the oven and preheat it to 400°F (200°C).
- In a food processor, pulse the wild nuts until finely chopped but not powdered.
- Season the fish fillets or chicken breasts with salt and pepper.
- Set up a breading station with three shallow bowls: one with flour, one with beaten eggs, and one with the chopped wild nuts.
- Dip each fish fillet or chicken breast into the flour, then into the beaten eggs, and finally into the chopped wild nuts, pressing gently to adhere.
- In a skillet over medium heat, warm the olive oil.
- Add the breaded fish or chicken and cook for a few minutes on each side until golden brown.
- Transfer the partially cooked fish or chicken to the prepared baking sheet and finish cooking in the preheated oven for about 10-15 minutes, or until cooked through and crispy.
- Serve the delicious wild nut-crusted fish or chicken as a flavorful and nutritious main dish.

Wild Nut and Green Salad

Ingredients: Assorted wild nuts (such as walnuts, pecans, or pine nuts), mixed salad greens, sliced fresh fruits (such as apples or pears), crumbled cheese (such as goat cheese or feta), vinaigrette dressing.

Instructions:
- Toast the wild nuts in a dry skillet over medium heat for a few minutes until fragrant and lightly browned.
- Take them out of the heat and let them cool.
- In a salad bowl, combine the mixed salad greens, sliced fresh fruits, crumbled cheese, and toasted wild nuts.
- Drizzle with your favorite vinaigrette dressing and toss gently to coat all the ingredients.
- Serve the wild nut and green salad as a refreshing and nutritious side dish or add grilled chicken or salmon to turn it into a satisfying main course.

Wild Nut-Crusted Goat Cheese

Ingredients: Assorted wild nuts (such as pistachios, almonds, or pecans), goat cheese rounds, honey, fresh herbs (such as thyme or rosemary), crackers or bread for serving.

Instructions:
- Place the wild nuts in a food processor and pulse until coarsely chopped.
- Roll each goat cheese round in the chopped wild nuts, pressing gently to adhere.

- Heat a skillet over medium heat and lightly toast the nut-crusted goat cheese rounds on each side for a minute or two, until the nuts are slightly golden and the cheese is warmed through.
- Transfer the nut-crusted goat cheese to a serving plate.
- Drizzle with honey and sprinkle with fresh herbs.
- Serve the warm and creamy nut-crusted goat cheese with crackers or bread as an elegant and flavorful appetizer.

Wild Nut Energy Bars

Ingredients: Assorted wild nuts (such as almonds, cashews, or hazelnuts), dates, dried fruits (such as apricots or figs), cocoa powder, coconut oil, honey or maple syrup, salt.

Instructions:
- In a food processor, blend the wild nuts, dates, dried fruits, cocoa powder, coconut oil, honey or maple syrup, and salt until the mixture comes together and forms a sticky dough.
- Spread parchment paper over a baking dish and press the mixture evenly into it.
- Place the dish in the refrigerator for at least 1 hour to set.

- Remove the chilled mixture from the dish and cut it into bars or squares.
- Store the wild nut energy bars in an airtight container in the refrigerator for a quick and nutritious snack.

Conclusion

This book provides a diverse collection of recipes showcasing the culinary uses of edible wild plants. From greens to underground vegetables, fruits and berries, seeds and grains, and nuts, each recipe offers a unique and flavorful experience.

By incorporating these wild plants into your cooking, you not only expand your culinary repertoire but also reap the nutritional benefits they offer. The recipes provide a rich source of vitamins, minerals, antioxidants, and fiber, promoting overall health and well-being.

From refreshing salads to hearty main courses and delightful snacks, these recipes offer a range of options to tantalize your taste buds and nourish your body. By embracing the abundance of edible wild plants, you can discover new flavors, textures, and healthful ingredients in your everyday meals.

Embrace the natural world and embark on a culinary journey with these recipes, celebrating the beauty and benefits of incorporating edible wild plants into your cooking. Discover the joys of foraging and savor the delicious and nutritious creations that await you.

ENJOY!!!

Printed in Great Britain
by Amazon